In the Nick Time™

HOUSE of WHITE BIRCHES
PUBLISHERS SINCE 1947

Table of Contents

Polka-Dot Christmas, page 4

- **4** Polka-Dot Christmas
- **7** Sassy Stiletto
- **11** Jingle Bells
- **15** Merry Miters
- **17** Oh Christmas Tree
- **23** Baby's First Christmas
- **27** Papa, Mama & Baby Bear
- **31** A Victorian Christmas
- **34** General Instructions

Sassy Stiletto, page 7

Jingle Bells, page 11

Introduction

Do you love the idea of knitting the night away during the holidays without a care in the world? Of course you do! If you're looking to deck those halls, then *In the Nick of Time* offers eight irresistible Christmas stocking patterns for the entire family.

The projects within cover sock knitting methods including the traditional cuff-down technique and the ever popular toe-up technique. Some highlights include a chunky cuff-down stocking that you can make in a snap, a playful sassy stiletto boot perfect for the beginner, and a traditional Victorian-era—inspired stocking.

In the Nick of Time offers a selection of patterns that are suitable for the novice who is ready to move on to in-the-round knitting, or who has tried her or his hand at sock knitting and other types of in-the-round knitting. From whimsical to the traditional, there's something for everyone to enjoy!

House of White Birches, Berne, Indiana 46711   AnniesAttic.com

Polka-Dot Christmas

Design by Sara Louise Harper

Embellish this quick, easy Christmas stocking with multicolored felted polka dots, and you have the perfect stocking for children and teens!

Skill Level

 INTERMEDIATE

Finished Size
Approx 16-inch circumference x 22 inches long (excluding hanging loop)

Materials
- Brown Sheep Burley Spun (chunky weight; 100% wool; 130 yds/226g per skein): 2 skeins kiwi #BS191 (MC)
- Plymouth Yarn Galway Worsted (worsted weight; 100% wool; 210 yds/100g per ball): 1 ball each plum #13 (A), orange #91 (B), fuchsia #163 (C) and yellow #179 (D)
- Size 8 (5mm) straight needles
- Size 13 (9mm) double-point needles (set of 5) or size needed to obtain gauge
- Stitch marker
- Stitch holders

Gauge
10 sts and 13 rnds = 4 inches/10cm in St st with larger needles and MC.
To save time, take time to check gauge.

Special Abbreviations
Make 1 (M1): Insert LH needle from front to back under horizontal strand between last st worked and next st on LH needle, k1-tbl.

N1, N2, N3, N4: Needle 1, Needle 2, Needle 3, Needle 4

Pattern Stitch
Double Rib
Rnd 1: *K2, p2; rep from * around.
Rep Rnd 1 for pat.

Pattern Notes
This stocking is worked in the round on double-point needles.

Polka dots are worked flat, felted, and then are sewn onto stocking.

Stocking
Cuff
With MC and larger needles, cast on 40 sts. Distribute evenly on 4 needles. Place marker for beg of rnd and join, taking care not to twist sts.

Work in Double Rib pat until cuff measures 6 inches.

Leg
Work in St st until leg measures 11 inches or desired length to heel.

Next rnd: K10, place next 20 sts (instep sts) on holder. Turn to work heel flap.

Heel flap
Working on heel sts only, p20, turn.

Row 1 (RS): Sl 1k, knit across.

Row 2: Sl 1p, purl across.

Rep [Rows 1 and 2] 6 times.

Turn heel
With RS facing, sl 1k, k12, ssk, turn.

Row 1 (WS): Sl 1p, p6, p2tog, turn, leaving rem sts unworked.

Row 2 (RS): Sl 1k, k6, ssk, turn, leaving rem sts unworked.

Rep Rows 1 and 2 until all sts have been worked—8 sts.

Next row: Purl across, turn.

Gusset
Set-up rnd: With N1, k8 heel sts, then pick up and knit 10 sts along edge of heel flap; with N2, k20 instep sts; with N3, pick up and knit 10 sts along edge of heel flap, then k4 heel sts from N1—48 sts.

Place marker for beg of rnd.

Rnd 1: N1: Knit to last 2 sts, k2tog; N2: Knit across; N3: Ssk, knit to end of rnd.

Rnd 2: Knit around.

Rep [Rnds 1 and 2] 3 times—40 sts.

Knit 7 rnds.

Toe
Rnd 1: N1: Knit to last 2 sts, k2tog; N2: Ssk, knit to last 2 sts, k2tog; N3: Ssk, knit to end.

Rnd 2: Knit around.

Rep [Rnds 1 and 2] 5 times—16 sts.

With N3, knit across sts on N1. Cut yarn leaving a 16-inch tail.

Finishing
Graft toe using Kitchener st. Weave in all ends.

Hanging loop
With 2 dpn and MC, cast on 3 sts. *K3, do not turn, slide sts to other end of needle, pull yarn across back of work; rep from * until I-cord measures approx 10 inches.

Next row: K1, k2tog, pass knit st over. Cut yarn and pull through final st.

Sew ends tog. Fold down cuff and attach ends of loop to inside of cuff.

Polka Dots
With smaller needles and desired color worsted weight, cast on 5 sts.

Row 1 (RS): Knit across.

Row 2: Purl across.

Row 3: K1, M1, k1, M1, k2, M1, k1—8 sts.

Row 4: P2, M1, p4, M1, p2—10 sts.

Row 5: K1, M1, k9—11 sts.

Rows 6, 8, 10 and 12: Purl across.

Row 7: K1, M1, k9, M1, k1—13 sts.

Row 9: K1, ssk, k7, k2tog, k1—11 sts.

Row 11: K1, ssk, k5, k2tog, k1—9 sts.

Row 13: K1, ssk, k1, k2tog, pass knit st over, k2tog, k1—5 sts.

Row 14: P1, p3tog, p1—3 sts.

Row 15: K1, k2tog, pass knit st over. Cut yarn, and pull through final st.

Work dots as desired in A, B, C and D, and felt by hand.

Hand-Felting
Vigorously scrub each dot in soapy water, alternating between hot and cold water. Shape and allow to dry thoroughly.

Attach dots as desired to stocking using a whip-stitch or stitch of your choice with matching or contrasting yarn. ❖

Sassy Stiletto

Design by Lisa Ellis

This high-fashion stiletto-boot stocking is a must for shoe and fashion aficionados. Beads are sewn on after completion.

Skill Level
INTERMEDIATE

Finished Size
Approx 18-inch cuff circumference x 17 inches long (excluding hanging loop)

Materials
- Plymouth Encore Worsted (worsted weight; 75% acrylic/25% wool; 200 yds/100g per ball): 1 ball fuchsia #1385 (A)
- Le Fibre Nobili and Lane Cervinia Imperiale (worsted weight; 80% mohair/20% nylon; 109 yds/25g per ball): 1 ball purple #4120 (B)
- Size 7 (4.5mm) double-point needles (set of 5) or size needed to obtain gauge
- Stitch markers
- Invisible sewing thread
- Thin sewing needle
- 100 (4mm) bicone glass beads

Gauge
21 sts and 28 rows = 4 inches/10cm in St st with A. To save time, take time to check gauge.

Special Abbreviation
Make 1 (M1): Insert LH needle from front to back under horizontal thread between the last st worked and next st on LH needle, k1-tbl.

Special Technique
3-Needle Bind-Off: Hold with WS tog and 2 needles parallel. Using a 3rd needle, knit tog 1 st from the front needle with 1 from the back. *Knit tog 1 st from the front with 1 st from back needle, and slip the first st over the 2nd to bind off. Rep from * until all sts are worked, then fasten off last st.

Pattern Notes
Stocking is worked from the cuff down. Increases and decreases shape the toe of the boot.

Beads are strung onto invisible thread and sewn onto the finished stocking.

If desired, additional beads can used to add a monogram to the cuff.

House of White Birches, Berne, Indiana 46711 AnniesAttic.com

Stocking

Cuff
With B, cast on 80 sts; divide evenly onto 4 dpn. Place marker for beg of rnd and join, taking care not to twist sts.

Work in rev St st for 5½ inches. Cut B.

Leg
Change to A and work in St st for 5 inches.

Calf shaping
Rnd 1: K1, k2tog, knit to last 2 sts, ssk.

Rnds 2–4: Knit around.

Rep [Rnds 1–4] 9 times—60 sts.

Continue in St st until leg measures 14 inches.

Next rnd: Knit to last 8 sts, place last 8 sts and first 8 sts of next rnd onto waste yarn for heel (to be worked later). Place marker and join, pulling yarn tight for beg of rnd.

Boot shaping
Set-up rnd: Knit, placing a marker between 22nd and 23rd sts to mark center toe—44 sts.

Rnd 1: K1, k2tog, knit to toe marker, M1, slip marker, k1, M1, knit to last 2 sts, ssk.

Rnd 2: K1, k2tog, knit to last 2 sts, ssk.

Rnd 3: Knit around.

Rep [Rnds 1–3] 4 times—34 sts total (17 sts between markers).

Toe shaping
Rnd 1: K1, k2tog, knit to toe marker, M1, slip marker, k1, M1, knit to last 2 sts, ssk.

Rnd 2: Knit to center toe marker, M1, slip toe marker, k1, M1, knit to end.

Rnd 3: Knit around.

Rep [Rnds 1–3] twice—40 sts total (20 sts between markers).

Place first 20 sts on 1 dpn, place last 20 sts on a 2nd dpn and join toe using 3-Needle Bind-Off.

Heel
Place 16 heel sts from waste yarn back onto 3 dpn. Join A and pick up 1 additional st at gap by toe to avoid a hole, join—17 sts.

Work in St st for 3 inches.

Next rnd: K2tog, k15—16 sts.

Place first 8 sts onto dpn and rem 8 sts on a 2nd dpn, and join heel tog using 3-Needle Bind-Off.

Hanging loop
With A, cast on 2 sts. *K2, do not turn, slip sts back to LH needle, pull yarn across back of work; rep from * until cord is approx 3 inches long. Bind off.

Join ends of I-cord to form loop and attach sewn ends to top of stocking inside cuff on heel side.

Finishing
With invisible thread and a sewing needle, sew 1 bead to each cast-on st along bottom of cuff—80 beads.

String 20 beads onto another length of thread and attach to stocking in a loop form, just below hanging loop. Weave in all ends. Block. ❖

Jingle Bells

Design by Ann Squire

Knit in a bright, self-striping yarn and decorated with gold bells, this easy-to-make stocking is sure to brighten your holidays. The thick, felted fabric is sturdy enough to hold lots of gifts!

Skill Level
INTERMEDIATE

Finished Size
16-inch circumference x 17 inches long (after felting, excluding hanging loop)

Materials
- Noro Kureyon (worsted weight; 100% wool; 110 yds/50g per ball): 4 balls red/teal/olive/magenta print #226
- 2 size 10½ (6.5 mm) 24-inch circular needles or double-point needles (set of 5) or size needed to obtain gauge
- 7 stitch markers
- 6 (¾-inch-diameter) gold jingle bells
- Pillowcase or mesh laundry bag for felting

Gauge
10 sts and 14 rnds = 4 inches/10cm in St st before felting.
Gauge is not critical for this project.

Special Abbreviations
Knit in front and back of stitch (kfb): Insert RH needle into front of st and knit as usual, but do not remove from LH needle; insert RH needle in back of same st and knit again removing from LH needle.

Wrap/Turn (W/T): Work to st indicated, *on RS rows*, bring yarn between needles to front of work, slip next st to RH needle, take yarn to back, slip wrapped st back to LH needle and turn; *on WS rows*, take yarn between needles to back, slip next st to RH needle, bring yarn between needles to front, slip wrapped st back to LH needle and turn.

Pattern Note
Stocking is worked in the round. It may be worked using either the double-point-needle or 2-circular-needle method.

Stocking

Toe
Cast on 6 sts; distribute sts onto 4 dpn, *or* if using 2 circular needles, place 3 sts on each needle. Place marker for beg of rnd and join, taking care not to twist sts.

Rnd 1: Knit.

Rnd 2: Kfb of each st—12 sts.

Rnd 3: K1, place marker, [k2, place marker] 5 times, k1.

Rnd 4: Kfb, slip marker, [k1, kfb, slip marker] 5 times, k1—18 sts.

Rnd 5: Knit.

Rnd 6: *Knit to st before marker, kfb, slip marker; rep from * to last st, k1—24 sts.

Rep [Rnds 5 and 6] 8 times—72 sts.

Next rnd: Knit around removing all but beg marker.

Work in St st until foot measures 9 inches from beg.

Heel
Heel is worked in rows on 36 heel sts only. Leave rem sts on 2 dpn *or* the other circular needle.

Row 1: Knit to last st, W/T.

Row 2: Purl to last st, W/T.

Row 3: Knit to st before last wrapped st, W/T.

Row 4: Purl to st before last wrapped st, W/T.

Rows 5–22: Rep [Rows 3 and 4] 9 times.

Note: There are 11 wrapped sts at each end of row and 14 unwrapped sts in the center.

Next row: Sl 1, knit to first wrapped st (11th st from end of row), knit wrapped st, W/T.

Note: This st and all subsequent wrapped sts will now have 2 wraps.

Next row: Sl 1, purl to first wrapped st (11th st from end of row), purl wrapped st, W/T.

Next row: Sl 1, knit to first double-wrapped st, knit double-wrapped st, W/T.

Next row: Sl 1, purl to first double-wrapped st, purl double-wrapped st, W/T.

Rep last 2 rows until 1 double-wrapped st rem at each end of work.

Next row: Sl 1, knit to double-wrapped st, knit double-wrapped st. Do not turn work. Place marker and join to work in rnds.

Leg
Work in St st for an additional 16 inches. On last rnd, place marker at center back of stocking.

Cuff
Rnd 1: *K11, kfb; rep from * around—78 sts.

Rnd 2: Knit around. Remove marker.

Shape points
Row 1: K13, turn.

Note: Work back and forth on these 13 sts. Double-point needles may be used, if desired.

Row 2: Purl across.

Row 3: K1, ssk, knit across—12 sts.

Row 4: P1, p2tog, purl across—11 sts.

Row 5: Knit across.

Row 6: P1, p2tog, purl across—10 sts.

Row 7: K1, ssk, knit across—9 sts.

Row 8: Purl across.

Rows 9–14: Rep Rows 3–8—5 sts.

Rows 15 and 16: Rep Rows 3 and 4—3 sts.

Row 17: Sl 1, k2tog, psso. Break yarn and pull through rem st.

Join yarn and rep Rows 1–17 for rem points.

Finishing
Weave in all ends and close hole in toe.

I-Cord hanging loop
With dpn, cast on 4 sts. *K4, slide sts to other end of needle, pull yarn across back of work; rep from * until I-cord is 6 inches long.

Next row: K1, k2tog, pass knit st over; pull yarn through final st.

Sew ends tog. If felted loop is desired, attach to inside of stocking at center back (in between the points)

Felting
Insert plastic bags into toe and leg of stocking to prevent these areas from felting together. Place stocking in pillowcase or mesh bag; close securely. Refer to page 40 for more information about felting. ❖

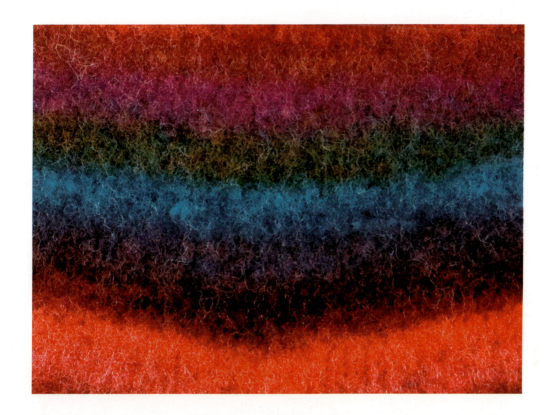

House of White Birches, Berne, Indiana 46711   AnniesAttic.com

Merry Miters

Design by Amy Polcyn

Worked from the toe up, this stocking includes a band of mitered squares and unusual (but easy) toe and heel shaping.

Skill Level
 EASY

Finished Size
Approx 10-inch circumference x 17 inches long (excluding hanging loop)

Materials

- Plymouth Yarn Trabajos del Peru (chunky weight; 100% merino wool; 147 yds/100g per skein): 1 skein each red/blue multi #10 (A) and blue #1 (B)
- Size 8 (5mm) double-point needles (set of 5) or size needed to obtain gauge
- Size H/8 (5mm) crochet hook
- Split-ring markers
- Stitch holder

Gauge
16 sts and 20 rnds = 4 inches/10cm in St st.
To save time, take time to check gauge.

Special Abbreviations
Knit in front and back (kfb): Knit in the front and back of next st to inc 1 st.

Central Double Decrease (CDD): Slip next 2 sts as if to k2tog, k1, p2sso to dec 2 sts.

Pattern Notes
Stocking is worked from the toe to cuff, beginning with a provisional cast-on.

The mitered squares are worked separately and sewn in place.

Slip all stitches as if to purl unless otherwise indicated.

Stocking

Toe
With waste yarn and crochet hook, ch 8. Fasten off.

With A, dpns and leaving an 8-inch tail, pick up and knit 6 sts, working 1 st in each loop of chain, leaving 1 chain on each end unworked. The waste yarn will be removed later.

Next row: Kfb in each st—12 sts.

Divide sts evenly on 4 dpns. Place marker for beg of rnd and join, being careful not to twist the sts.

Rnd 1: Knit around.

Rnd 2: *Kfb, k2; rep from * around—16 sts.

Rnd 3: Knit around.

Rnd 4: *Kfb, knit to end of needle; rep from * around (4 sts inc).

Rep [Rnds 3 and 4] 5 times—40 sts.

Foot
Work even in St st until foot measures 6 inches from beg.

House of White Birches, Berne, Indiana 46711 AnniesAttic.com

Heel

Work back and forth in rows on 20 sts for heel only. Place rem 20 sts for instep on holder.

Row 1 (RS): Sl 1, knit to last st, turn.

Row 2: Sl 1, purl to last st, turn.

Row 3: Sl 1, knit to last 2 sts, turn.

Row 4: Sl 1, purl to last 2 sts, turn.

Row 5: Sl 1, knit to last 3 sts, turn.

Row 6: Sl 1, purl to last 3 sts, turn.

Row 7: Sl 1, knit to last 4 sts, turn.

Row 8: Sl 1, purl to last 4 sts, turn.

Row 9: Sl 1, knit to last 5 sts, turn.

Row 10: Sl 1, purl to last 5 sts, turn.

Row 11: Sl 1, knit to last 6 sts, turn.

Row 12: Sl 1, purl to last 6 sts, turn.

Note: There are now 6 unworked sts at each end and 8 sts in the center. On 2nd half of heel, each of the unworked sts is worked tog with a purl bump picked up from the row below.

Next row (RS): Sl 1, knit to last 6 sts, slip next st as if to knit, with tip of RH needle lift purl bump of next st on row below (from the WS) and place on needle; ssk the slipped st and lifted st tog, turn.

Next row: Sl 1, purl to last 6 sts, with tip of needle lift purl bump of previous st on row below and place on LH needle, p2tog using the lifted st and the next st on LH needle, turn.

Continue as established, working to next unworked st and working it with lifted purl bump until all sts have been worked. On last RS row, lift st from edge of heel.

Leg

Work in St st on heel and instep sts until leg measures 12 inches from base of heel. Bind off loosely.

Mitered square
Make 4

With B, cast on 21 sts, placing marker on center (11th) st.

Row 1 (RS): Knit across.

Row 2: Knit to st before marked st, CDD, knit to end.

Rep [Rows 1 and 2] until 3 sts rem.

Next row: K3tog. Fasten off.

Sew mitered squares tog to form a strip. Sew strip in place along top edge of stocking.

I-Cord trim

With A, cast on 3 sts. *K3, slide sts to opposite end of needle, pull yarn across back of work; rep from * until I-cord measures approx 16 inches.

Next row: Sl 1, k2tog, psso. Fasten off.

Finishing

Beg and ending at heel, sew I-cord in place along top edge of stocking, creating a hanging loop from excess length at of I-cord.

Remove waste yarn from toe, placing "live" sts on needle. Thread yarn tail through the 6 live sts and pull tight to close.

Weave in ends, block. ❖

Oh Christmas Tree

Design by Amy Marshall

This whimsical intarsia stocking, knit in bold red, gold and green, gives this design a traditional touch.

Skill Level
 INTERMEDIATE

Finished Size
Approx 13-inch circumference x 17 inches long (excluding hanging loop)

Materials
- Berroco Comfort (worsted weight; 50% nylon/50% acrylic; 210 yds/100g per ball): 1 ball each primary red #9750 (MC), lovage #9761 (A), Spanish brown #9727 (B) and barley #9703 (C)
- Size 9 (5.5mm) straight and double-point needles (set of 4) or size needed to obtain gauge
- Size 8 (5mm) straight needle
- Stitch markers (optional)
- Bobbins (optional)

Gauge
16 sts and 22 rows = 4 inches/10cm in St st.
To save time, take time to check gauge.

Special Abbreviation
Wrap/Turn (W/T): Work to st indicated, *on RS rows*, bring yarn between needles to front of work, slip next st to RH needle, take yarn to back, slip wrapped st back to LH needle and turn; *on WS rows*, take yarn between needles to back, slip next st to RH needle, bring yarn between needles to front, slip wrapped st back to LH needle and turn.

Special Technique
Knit Cast-On: Make a slip knot on LH needle, *insert RH needle into loop on LH needle and k1; without slipping loop off needle place new st from RH needle on LH needle; rep from * for desired number of sts.

Pattern Note
When working pattern from chart, use intarsia technique, winding small balls or bobbins for each colored section, and bringing new color under and around previous color to lock in place and avoid holes.

Stocking

Hem
With larger straight needles and A, and using knit cast-on, cast on 54 sts.

Work in St st until piece measures approx 1½ inches ending with a RS row. → ending after K

Next row (turning ridge): Knit across. Cut A.

Leg
Join MC and continue in St st until piece measures approx 3 inches from cast-on edge, ending with a WS row. ending after P

Note: If desired, cast-on loops may be picked up on a needle 1 size smaller and knit tog with working sts to join hem on next row.

Next row (joining hem): Fold up the hem along turning ridge with WS tog, and MC sts in front. *Insert RH needle into next st on LH needle and then into loop of corresponding cast-on st behind and k2tog; rep from * until all sts are worked and hem is secured in place.

Next row: Purl across.

Place markers after st 17 and after st 37.

Continue in St st until piece measures approx 1¾ inches from turning ridge, ending with a WS row.

Work Rows 1–50 of chart between markers.

Remove markers and continue St st in MC only until leg measures approx 10½ inches.

Divide onto evenly onto 3 dpn. Place marker and join to work in rnds. → ending after P

Continue in St st until leg measures approx 11 inches.

Heel
Heel is worked in rows on 27 heel sts only. Leave rem sts on 2 dpn for instep.

Row 1 (RS): With A, knit to last st, W/T.

Row 2: Purl to last st, W/T.

19/10/2011 purl → & wrapped

Row 3: Knit to last 2 sts, W/T.

Row 4: Purl to last 2 sts, W/T.

Row 5: Knit to last 3 sts, W/T.

Row 6: Purl to last 3 sts, W/T.

Row 7: Knit to last 4 sts, W/T.

Row 8: Purl to last 4 sts, W/T.

Row 9: Knit to last 5 sts, W/T.

Row 10: Purl to last 5 sts, W/T.

Row 11: Knit to last 6 sts, W/T.

Row 12: Purl to last 6 sts, W/T.

Note: There are 6 wrapped sts at each end of row and 15 unwrapped sts in the center.

Row 13: Sl 1p, knit to first wrapped st (6th st from end of row), lift wrap and knit tog with wrapped st, turn.

Row 14: Sl 1p, purl to first wrapped st (6th st from end of row), lift wrap and purl tog with wrapped st, turn.

Row 15: Sl 1p, knit to wrapped st, lift wrap and knit tog with wrapped st, turn.

Row 16: Sl 1p, purl to wrapped st, lift wrap and purl tog with wrapped st, turn.

Continue in same manner until all wrapped sts have been worked—27 sts.

House of White Birches, Berne, Indiana 46711   AnniesAttic.com

Instep
With MC, work in St st in rnds on heel and instep sts until instep measures approx 4 inches.

Toe
With A, work 1 rnd, placing markers for beg of rnd and after 27th st.

Dec rnd: *K1, k2tog, knit to 3 sts before marker, ssk, k1, slip marker; rep from * around—50 sts (4 sts dec).

Rep [Dec rnd] 9 times—12 sts.

Finishing
Divide sts onto 2 needles and graft to using Kitchener st.

Sew leg seam using mattress st and half-st seam allowance.

Weave in all ends.

I-Cord hanger
With A and dpn, cast on 4 sts. *K4, slide sts to other end of needle, pull yarn across back of work; rep from * until I-cord is 3 inches long.

Sew ends tog and sew to inside back seam. ❖

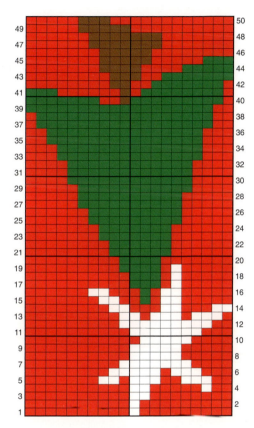

OH CHRISTMAS TREE CHART

STITCH KEY
- ■ (MC) k on RS, p on WS
- ■ (A) k on RS, p on WS
- ■ (B) k on RS, p on WS
- □ (C) k on RS, p on WS

Baby's First Christmas

Design by Sara Louise Harper

What a wonderfully soft stocking for Baby's first Christmas!

Skill Level
 INTERMEDIATE

Finished Size
Approx 12-inch circumference x 18 inches long (excluding hanging loop)

Materials
- Plymouth Yarn Baby Alpaca DK (DK weight, 100% baby alpaca; 125 yds/50g per ball): 1 ball each natural #100 (A), dusty pink #1837 (B) and dusty yellow #1104 (C)
- Size 6 (4mm) double-point needles (set of 4) and 16-inch circular (optional) or size needed to obtain gauge
- Size C/2 (2.75mm) crochet hook
- Stitch markers
- Stitch holders

Gauge
23 sts and 30 rnds = 4 inches/10cm in St st with A. To save time, take time to check gauge.

Special Abbreviation
N1, N2, N3: Needle 1, Needle 2, Needle 3

Pattern Stitches
Double Rib
Rnd 1: *K2, p2; rep from * around.
Rep Rnd 1 for pat.

Seed St
Rnd 1: *K1, p1; rep from * around.
Rnd 2: Purl the knit sts and knit the purl sts around.
Rep Rnd 2 for pat.

Pattern Note
Instructions are given for working this stocking in rounds with double-point needles. If preferred, cuff, leg and foot of stocking can be worked on a short (16-inch) circular needle by placing stitch markers to indicate where individual double-point needles would be used.

Stocking

Cuff
With B, cast on 68 sts and divide onto 3 dpn. Place marker to indicate beg of rnd and join, being careful not to twist sts.

Work in Double Rib pat until cuff measures 3½ inches. Cut yarn.

Leg
Change to A and work 2 rnds in St st, and then work 2 rnds in seed st.

Set-up diagonal seed pat: Work 33 sts in seed st pat, place marker, k2, place marker, work in seed st pat to end of rnd.

Work 32 sts in seed st pat, slip next st, remove marker, slip st back to LH needle, replace marker, k3, remove marker, knit next st, then replace marker; work to end of rnd.

Continue in this manner, working 2 additional sts in St st between markers and 2 less sts in seed st pat on each rnd. When all seed sts have been worked into St st pat, work even in St st until leg measures 10½ inches from cast-on edge. Cut yarn.

Heel flap
With B, k17, turn. P34 for heel and place rem sts on holders for instep.

Row 1 (RS): Sl 1k, knit across.

Row 2: Sl 1p, purl across.

Rep [Rows 1 and 2] 12 times.

Turn heel
Row 1 (RS): Sl 1k, k19, ssk, k1, turn, leaving rem 11 sts unworked.

Row 2 (WS): Sl 1p, p7, p2tog, p1, turn, leaving rem 11 sts unworked.

Row 3: Sl 1k, k8, ssk, k1, turn, leaving rem 9 sts unworked.

Row 4: Sl 1p, p9, p2tog, p1, turn, leaving rem 9 sts unworked.

Row 5: Sl 1k, k10, ssk, k1, turn, leaving rem 7 sts unworked.

Row 6: Sl 1p, p11, p2tog, p1, turn, leaving rem 7 sts unworked.

Continue in this manner slipping first st, working to 1 st before gap, working 2 sts tog, working 1 st, and then turning until 20 sts rem on needle, ending with a WS row.

Knit across 10 sts; cut yarn.

Gusset

Set-up rnd: With N1 and A, k10 rem heel sts, then pick up and knit 14 sts along side of heel flap; with N2, knit across 34 instep sts on holders; with N3, pick up and knit 14 sts along side of heel flap, then knit across 10 heel sts; place marker for beg of rnd—82 sts.

Rnd 1: N1: K1, [p1, k1] across to last 3 sts, k2tog, k1; N2: [P1, k1] across; N3: K1, ssk, k1, [p1, k1] to end of rnd.

Rnd 2: N1: P1, [k1, p1] to last 2 sts, k2; N2: [K1, p1] across; N3: K2, work in seed st pat to end of rnd.

Rnd 3: N1: Work in seed st pat to last 3 sts, k2tog, k1; N2: Work in seed st pat across; N3: K1, ssk, work in seed st pat to end of rnd.

Rnd 4: N1: Work in seed st pat to last 2 sts, k2; N2: Work in seed st pat across; N3: K2, work in seed st pat to end of rnd.

Rep [Rnds 3 and 4] 5 times—68 sts (N1—17 sts, N2—34 sts, N3—17 sts).

Work even in seed st pat until foot measures 4 inches from picked up sts (or 3 inches less than desired length to toe).

Next rnd: Knit around. Cut yarn.

Next rnd: With B, knit around.

Reverse Side of Stocking

Toe

Rnd 1: N1: Knit to last 3 sts, k2tog, k1; N2: K1, ssk, knit to last 3 sts, k2tog, k1; N3: K1, ssk, knit to end of rnd—64 sts.

Rnd 2: Knit around.

Rep [Rnds 1 and 2] 6 times—40 sts.

Rep [Rnd 1] 4 times—24 sts.

With N3, knit all sts on N1.

Cut yarn leaving a 16-inch tail, and graft toe tog with Kitchener st. Weave in all ends.

Finishing

I-Cord hanging loop

With B, cast on 3 sts. *K3, do not turn, slide sts to other end of needle, pull yarn across back of work; rep from * until I-cord measures approx 8 inches.

Next row: K1, k2tog, pass knit st over; pull yarn through final st.

Sew ends tog, then attach to inside of stocking cuff at back.

Weave in all ends and block stretching ribbing as desired.

Embellishing

With C and crochet hook, work crochet chains below ribbing, outlining color areas and down diagonal line of seed st pat area.

Write "Baby" or baby's name using duplicate st or crochet chain, accenting each letter with a French knot.

Embellish stocking's reverse side as shown in photo or as desired.

To work crochet chain: With crochet hook and yarn inside stocking, pull a st through to top of stocking with hook; pull a 2nd st through, then pull 2nd st through first to form chain. Rep to cover desired area.

To make a French knot: Come up at top right of st, wrap yarn around tapestry needle 3 times, then go down 1 thread away. ❖

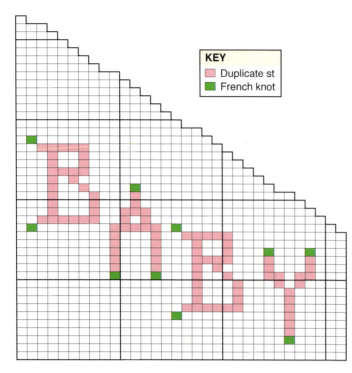

BABY'S FIRST CHRISTMAS CHART

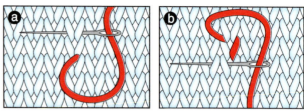

DUPLICATE STITCH

From underneath piece, bring yarn up in the center of the st below the st to be duplicated. Place needle from right to left behind both sides of the st above the one being duplicated, and pull yarn through (a). Complete the st by returning the needle to where you began (b).

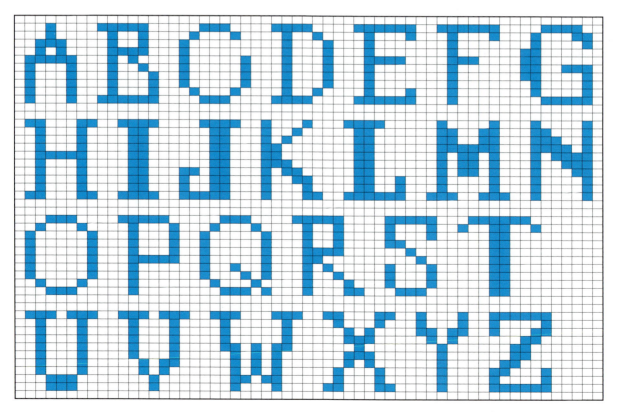

DUPLICATE-STITCH ALPHABET CHART

Papa, Mama & Baby Bear

Design by Lisa Ellis

Cozy up by the fire to make these quick-to-knit stockings—they're perfect for the whole family!

Skill Level

 INTERMEDIATE

Sizes
Small (medium, large) Instructions are given for smallest size, with larger sizes in parentheses. When only 1 number is given, it applies to all sizes.

Finished Measurements
14- (22-, 22-) inch cuff circumference x 10 (15½, 20) inches long (excluding hanging loop)

Materials
- Plymouth Encore Mega (super chunky; 75% acrylic/25% wool; 64 yds/100g per ball): 1 (3, 3) balls off-white #256
- Size 13 (9.0mm) double-point needles (set of 5) and 16-inch circular needle (optional for sizes medium and large) or size needed to obtain gauge
- Stitch markers, 1 in CC for beg of rnd
- Cable needle

Gauge
10 sts and 14 rnds = 4 inches/10cm in St st. To save time, take time to check gauge.

Special Abbreviations
2 over 2 Left Cross (2/2 LC): Slip next 2 sts to cn and hold to front of work; k2, k2 from cn.

N1, N2, N3, N4: Needle 1, Needle 2, Needle 3, Needle 4

Pattern Stitches
Double Moss (multiple of 4 sts in the rnd)
Rnds 1 and 2: *K2, p2; rep from * around.
Rnds 3 and 4: *P2, k2; rep from * around.
Rep Rnds 1–4 for pat.

Cable (multiple of 6 sts in the rnd)
Rnd 1: P1, k4, *p2, k4; rep from * to last st, p1.
Rnds 2–8: Rep Rnd 1.
Rnd 9: P1, 2/2 LC, *p2, 2/2 LC; rep from * to last st, p1.
Rep Rnds 1–9 for pat.

Instep Cable (multiple of 6 sts in the rnd)
Rnd 1: K5, *p2, k4; rep from * to last st, k1.
Rnds 2–8: Rep Rnd 1.
Rnd 9: K1, 2/2 LC, *p2, 2/2 LC; rep from * to last st, k1.
Rep Rnds 1–9 for pat.

Pattern Notes
Stockings are knit in the round from the cuff to the toe with a heel flap and gusset.

If desired, the medium and large stockings may be worked using a 16-inch circular needle for the cuff and leg.

Small stocking is worked on double-point needles throughout.

Stocking

Cuff
Cast on 28 (40, 40) sts, dividing evenly onto 4 dpn. Place marker for beg of rnd and join, taking care not to twist sts.

Work [Rnds 1–4 of Double Moss pat] 3 (3, 4) times.

Leg
Work in St st for 2½ (3, 3½) inches.

Next rnd: Knit around, inc 8 sts evenly—36 (48, 48) sts.

For Small & Medium Sizes
Work Rnds 2–9 of Cable pat.

For Large Size
Work Rnds 4–9 of Cable pat.

For All Sizes
Work [Rnds 1–9 of Cable pat] 0 (1, 2) times, and then rep Rnds 1–3 of Cable pat.

Heel flap
Row 1 (RS): Sl 1, k4, [p2, k4] 2 (3, 3) times, k1, turn, leaving rem sts unworked.

Row 2: Sl 1p, p4, [k2, p4] 2 (3, 3) times, p1, turn—18 (24, 24) heel flap sts.

Rep [Rows 1 and 2] 4 (7, 8) times.

Heel turn
Row 1 (RS): K11 (14, 14) sts, skp, k1, turn, leaving rem 4 (7, 7) sts unworked.

Row 2 (WS): Sl 1p, p5, p2tog, p1, turn, leaving rem 4 (7, 7) sts unworked.

Row 3: Sl 1k, k6, skp, k1, turn, leaving rem 2 (5, 5) sts unworked.

Row 4: Sl 1p, p7, p2tog, p1, turn, leaving rem 2 (5, 5) sts unworked.

Row 5: Sl 1k, k8, skp, k0 (1, 1) sts turn, leaving rem 0 (3, 3) sts unworked.

Row 6: Sl 1, p9 (10, 10), p2tog, p0 (1, 1) st, turn—12 sts.

For Medium & Large Sizes
Row 7: Sl 1k, k10, skp, k1, turn, leaving rem st unworked.

Row 8: Sl 1p, p11, p2tog, p1, turn, leaving rem st unworked.

Row 9: Sl 1, k12, skp, turn.

Row 10: P12, p2tog, p1, turn—14 (14) sts.

Gusset
Set-up rnd: With N1, knit across first 6 (7, 7) heel sts; with N2, knit rem 6 (7, 7) heel sts; then pick up and knit 6 (7, 8) sts along the side of heel flap, place marker; with N3, work across instep in Instep Cable pat beg with Rnd 4; with N4, pick up and knit 6 (7, 8) sts along the other side of heel flap, place marker, then knit first 6 (7, 7) heel sts from N1; place CC marker to mark beg of rnd—12 (14, 15) sts each now on N1 and N3 for heel and 18 (24, 24) sts on N2 for instep.

Rnd 1: N1: Knit to last 3 sts, k2tog, k1; N2: Work Rnd 5 of Instep Cable pat; N3: K1, skp, knit to end of rnd.

Rep [Rnd 1] 2 (5, 2) times—36 (40, 48) sts.

Work even for 3 (5, 7) rnds, knitting sts on N1 and N3 and working in established Instep Cable pat on N2.

Toe shaping
For Medium & Large Sizes
Rnd 1: *K6, k2tog; rep from * around.

Rnd 2: *K5, k2tog; rep from * around.

For All Sizes
Rnd 1 (3, 3): *K4, k2tog; rep from * around.

Rnd 2 (4, 4): *K3, k2tog; rep from * around.

Rnd 3 (5, 5): *K2, k2tog; rep from * around.

Rnd 4 (6, 6): *K1, k2tog; rep from * around.

Rnd 5 (7, 7): *K2tog; rep from * around—6 (5, 6) sts.

Finishing
Cut yarn, leaving 10-inch tail. Weave tail through rem sts and pull tight to secure. Weave in all ends. Block.

Hanging loop
With dpn, cast on 2 sts. Work in garter st for 3 inches. Bind off loosely.

Sew ends of loop tog. Fold cuff down and sew loop inside cuff. ❖

House of White Birches, Berne, Indiana 46711   AnniesAttic.com

A Victorian Christmas

Design by Sara Louise Harper

This basic stocking adds a few festive flourishes—red and white stripes, an interesting "elf point" cuff and fun holly leaves with berries.

Skill Level
INTERMEDIATE

Finished Size
Approx 16-inch circumference x 22 inches long (excluding hanging loop)

Materials
- Cascade Yarns Cascade 220 Wool (worsted weight; 100% Peruvian highland wool; 220 yds/100g per hank): 1 hank each gold #2415 (A), white #8010 (B), red #9404 (C) and green #9428 (D)
- Size 7 (4.5mm) double-point needles (set of 4) and 16-inch circular needle (optional) or size needed to obtain gauge
- Stitch markers
- Stitch holders

Gauge
22 sts and 20 rnds = 4 inches/10cm in Stripe pat. To save time, take time to check gauge.

Special Abbreviations
Make 1 (M1): Insert LH needle from front to back under horizontal thread between last st worked and next st on LH needle, k1-tbl.

N1, N2, N3: Needle 1, Needle 2, Needle 3

Pattern Stitch
Stripe
Rnd 1: *K1 C, k3 B; rep from * around.
Rep Rnd 1 for pat.

Pattern Notes
Instructions are given for working this stocking in rounds with double-point needles. If preferred, cuff, leg and foot can be worked on a short (16-inch) circular needle by placing stitch markers to indicate where individual double-point needles would be used.

When working Stripe pattern, carry yarn loosely across back of work.

Stocking

Cuff
Elf Point

Make 8

With A, cast on 1 st.

Row 1: M1, k1—2 sts.

Row 2: M1, p2—3 sts.

Row 3: M1, knit across.

Row 4: M1, purl across.

Rep [Rows 3 and 4] 3 times—10 sts.

Cut yarn.

Note: After completing each point, slide it to end of needle. On final elf point do not cut yarn.

Next row: Purl across—80 sts.

Divide onto 3 dpns. Place marker for beg of rnd and join, being careful not to twist sts.

Work in St st until elf points measure 6 inches from tip of cast-on. Cut yarn.

Leg
Hold cuff with WS facing (WS of cuff becomes RS of leg) and work 12 inches in Strip pat. Cut yarns.

Heel flap
Next row: With A, k20 sts, turn.

Next row: P40 sts for heel and place rem sts on holders for instep.

Row 1 (RS): Sl 1k, *k1, sl 1; rep from * across to last st, k1.

Row 2: Sl 1p, purl across.

Rep [Rows 1 and 2] 14 times.

Turn heel
Row 1 (RS): Sl 1k, k22, ssk, k1, turn, leaving rem sts unworked.

Row 2 (WS): Sl 1p, p7, p2tog, p1, turn, leaving rem sts unworked.

Row 3: Sl 1k, k8, ssk, k1, turn, leaving rem sts unworked.

Row 4: Sl 1p, p9, p2tog, p1, turn, leaving rem sts unworked.

Continue in this manner slipping first st, working to 1 st before gap, working 2 sts tog, working next st, and then turning until 24 sts rem.

Gusset
Set-up rnd: With N1 and A, knit across 24 heel sts; then working along side of heel [with C pick up and knit 1 st, with B pick up and knit 3 sts] 4 times; with N2, work Stripe pat as established across 40 instep sts; with N3, pick up and knit 16 sts along side of heel continuing in established Stripe pat; then continue in established Stripe pat across first 12 sts on N1; place marker and join to work in rnds.

Rnd 1: N1: Work in Stripe pat to last 3 sts, k2tog, k1; N2: Work in Stripe pat across; N3: K1, ssk, work in Stripe pat to end of rnd.

Rnd 2: Work in established pat around.

Rep Rnds 1 and 2 until there are 20 sts on N1 and N3 and 40 sts on N2—80 sts.

Work even in pat until foot measures 5½ inches from picked-up sts or desired length. Cut yarn.

With A, work 2 rnds.

Toe
Rnd 1: N1: Knit to last 3 sts, k2tog, k1; N2: K1, ssk, knit to last 3 sts, k2tog, k1; N3: K1, ssk, knit to end.

Rnd 2: Knit.

Rep Rnds 1 and 2 until 48 sts rem.

Rep Rnd 1 until 24 sts rem.

With N3 knit sts on N1.

Cut yarn, leaving a 16-inch tail. Divide sts evenly onto 2 needles and graft toe tog using Kitchener st. Weave in all ends.

I-Cord hanging loop
With A, cast on 3 sts. *K3, do not turn, slide sts to other end of needle, pull yarn across back of work; rep from * until I-cord measures approx 8 inches.

Next row: K1, k2tog, pass knit st over, pull yarn through final st.

Sew ends tog. Sew to inside of stocking cuff at back.

Holly leaves
Make 2 or 3 as desired

With D, cast on 5 sts.

Work 2 rows in St st.

Row 1 (RS): K1, M1, k1, yo, k1, yo, k1, M1, k1—9 sts.

Rows 2, 4, 6, 10, 12, 16, 18: Purl across.

Rows 3 and 9: K4, yo, k1, yo, k4—11 sts.

Rows 5 and 11: K5, yo, k1, yo, k5—13 sts.

Row 7: Bind off 3 sts, k2, yo, k1, yo, k6—12 sts.

Row 8: Bind off 3 sts, p8—9 sts.

Row 13: Bind off 3 sts, k9—10 sts.

Row 14: Bind off 3 sts, p6—7 sts.

Row 15: Ssk, k3, k2tog—5 sts.

Row 17: Ssk, k1, k2tog—3 sts.

Row 19: Sl 1, k2tog, psso—1 st.

Fasten off.

Holly berries
Make 3

With C, cast on 1 st, leaving a 10-inch tail. Knit in front, back, front, back and front of st—5 sts.

Row 1: Knit across.

Row 2: Purl across.

Row 3: Knit across.

Row 4: P2tog, p1, p2tog—3 sts.

Row 5: Knit across.

Row 6: P3tog—1 st.

Fasten off, leaving a 10-inch tail.

With 1 tail, sew around outer edge of berry. Stuff 2nd tail inside and pull tight.

Finishing
Weave ends from elf points down each side of point to help stabilize.

Block stocking giving particular attention to elf points. Block holly leaves. When completely dry, sew holly leaves and berries to stocking as desired. ❖

General Instructions

Basic Stitches

Garter Stitch
On straight needles knit every row. When working in the round on circular or double-point needles, knit one round then purl one round.

Stockinette Stitch
On straight needles knit right-side rows and purl wrong-side rows. When working on circular or double-point needles, knit all rounds.

Reverse Stockinette Stitch
On straight needles purl right-side rows and knit wrong-side rows. On circular or double-point needles, purl all rounds.

Ribbing
Combines knit and purl stitches within a row to give stretch to the garment. Ribbing is most often used for the lower edge of the front and back, the cuffs and neck edge of garments.

The rib pattern is established on the first row. On subsequent rows the knit stitches are knitted and purl stitches are purled to form the ribs.

Reading Pattern Instructions
Before beginning a pattern, look through it to make sure you are familiar with the abbreviations that are used.

Some patterns may be written for more than one size. In this case the smallest size is given first and others are placed in parentheses. When only one number is given, it applies to all sizes.

You may wish to highlight the numbers for the size you are making before beginning. It is also helpful to place a self-sticking note on the pattern to mark any changes made while working the pattern.

Gauge
The single most important factor in determining the finished size of a knit item is the gauge. Although not as important for flat, one-piece items, it is important when making a clothing item that needs to fit properly.

It is important to make a stitch-gauge swatch about 4 inches square with recommended patterns and needles before beginning.

Measure the swatch. If the number of stitches and rows are fewer than indicated under "Gauge" in the pattern, your needles are too large. Try another swatch with smaller-size needles. If the number of stitches and rows are more than indicated under "Gauge" in the pattern, your needles are too small. Try another swatch with larger-size needles.

Continue to adjust needles until correct gauge is achieved.

Working From Charts
When working with more than one color in a row, sometimes a chart is provided to follow the pattern. On the chart each square represents one stitch. A key is given indicating the color or stitch represented by each color or symbol in the box.

When working in rows, odd-numbered rows are usually read from right to left, and even-numbered rows from left to right.

Odd-numbered rows represent the right side of the work and are usually knit. Even-numbered rows represent the wrong side and are usually purled.

When working in rounds, every row on the chart is a right-side row, and is read from right to left.

Glossary

bind-off—used to finish an edge

cast-on—process of making foundation stitches used in knitting

decrease—means of reducing the number of stitches in a row

increase—means of adding to the number of stitches in a row

intarsia—method of knitting a multicolored pattern into the fabric

knitwise—insert needle into stitch as if to knit

make 1—method of increasing using the strand between the last stitch worked and the next stitch

place marker—placing a purchased marker or loop of contrasting yarn onto the needle for ease in working a pattern repeat

purlwise—insert needle into stitch as if to purl

right side—side of garment or piece that will be seen when worn

selvage stitch—edge stitch used to make seaming easier

slip, slip, knit—method of decreasing by moving stitches from left needle to right needle and working them together

slip stitch—an unworked stitch slipped from left needle to right needle, usually as if to purl

wrong side—side that will be inside when garment is worn

work even—continue to work in the pattern as established without working any increases or decreases

work in pattern as established—continue to work following the pattern stitch as it has been set up or established on the needle, working any increases or decreases in such a way that the established pattern remains the same

yarn over—method of increasing by wrapping the yarn over the right needle without working a stitch

Standard Abbreviations

[ ] work instructions within brackets as many times as directed
( ) work instructions within parentheses in the place directed
** repeat instructions following the asterisks as directed
* repeat instructions following the single asterisk as directed
" inch(es)
approx approximately
beg begin/begins/beginning
CC contrasting color
ch chain stitch
cm centimeter(s)
cn cable needle
dec decrease/decreases/decreasing
dpn(s) double-point needle(s)
g gram(s)
inc increase/increases/increasing
k knit
k2tog knit 2 stitches together

kwise knitwise
LH left hand
m meter(s)
M1 make one stitch
MC main color
mm millimeter(s)
oz ounce(s)
p purl
pat(s) pattern(s)
p2tog purl 2 stitches together
psso pass slipped stitch over
p2sso pass 2 slipped stitches over
pwise purlwise
rem remain/remains/remaining
rep repeat(s)
rev St st reverse stockinette stitch
RH right hand
rnd(s) round(s)
RS right side

skp slip, knit, pass slipped stitch over—one stitch decreased
sk2p slip 1, knit 2 together, pass slip stitch over the knit 2 together—2 stitches have been decreased
sl slip
sl 1k slip 1 knitwise
sl 1p slip 1 purlwise
sl st slip stitch(es)
ssk slip, slip, knit these 2 stitches together—a decrease
st(s) stitch(es)
St st stockinette stitch/stocking stitch
tbl through back loop(s)
tog together
WS wrong side
wyib with yarn in back
wyif with yarn in front
yd(s) yard(s)
yfwd yarn forward
yo yarn over

House of White Birches, Berne, Indiana 46711 AnniesAttic.com

Knitting Basics

Cast-On
Leaving an end about an inch long for each stitch to be cast on, make a slip knot on the right needle.

Place the thumb and index finger of your left hand between the yarn ends with the long yarn end over your thumb, and the strand from the skein over your index finger. Close your other fingers over the strands to hold them against your palm. Spread your thumb and index fingers apart and draw the yarn into a "V."

Place the needle in front of the strand around your thumb and bring it underneath this strand. Carry the needle over and under the strand on your index finger.

Draw through loop on thumb.

Drop the loop from your thumb and draw up the strand to form a stitch on the needle.

Repeat until you have cast on the number of stitches indicated in the pattern. Remember to count the beginning slip knot as a stitch.

Cable Cast-On
This type of cast-on is used when adding stitches in the middle or at the end of a row.

Make a slip knot on the left needle. Knit a stitch in this knot and place it on the left needle. Insert the right needle between the last two stitches on the left needle. Knit a stitch and place it on the left needle. Repeat for each stitch needed.

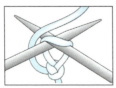
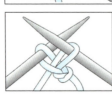

Knit (k)
Insert tip of right needle from front to back in next stitch on left needle.

Bring yarn under and over the tip of the right needle.

Pull yarn loop through the stitch with right needle point.

Slide the stitch off the left needle. The new stitch is on the right needle.

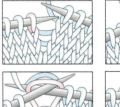
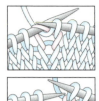

Purl (p)
With yarn in front, insert tip of right needle from back to front through next stitch on the left needle. Bring yarn around the right needle counterclockwise. With right needle, draw yarn back through the stitch.

Slide the stitch off the left needle. The new stitch is on the right needle.

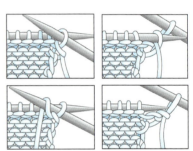

Bind-Off

Binding off (knit)
Knit first two stitches on left needle. Insert tip of left needle into first stitch worked on right needle and pull it over the second stitch and completely off the needle.

Knit the next stitch and repeat. When one stitch remains on right needle, cut yarn and draw tail through last stitch to fasten off.

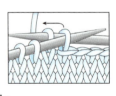

Binding off (purl)
Purl first two stitches on left needle. Insert tip of left needle into first stitch worked on right needle and pull it over the second stitch and completely off the needle.

Purl the next stitch and repeat. When one stitch remains on right needle, cut yarn and draw tail through last stitch to fasten off.

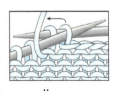

Increase (inc)

Two stitches in one stitch

Increase (knit)
Knit the next stitch in the usual manner, but don't remove the stitch from the left needle. Place right needle behind left needle and knit again into the back of the same stitch. Slip original stitch off left needle.

Increase (purl)
Purl the next stitch in the usual manner, but don't remove the stitch from the left needle. Place right needle behind left needle and purl again into the back of the same stitch. Slip original stitch off left needle.

Invisible Increase (M1)
There are several ways to make or increase one stitch.

Make 1 with Left Twist (M1L)
Insert left needle from front to back under the horizontal loop between the last stitch worked and next stitch on left needle.
  With right needle, knit into the back of this loop.
  To make this increase on the purl side, insert left needle in same manner and purl into the back of the loop.

Make 1 with Right Twist (M1R)
Insert left needle from back to front under the horizontal loop between the last stitch worked and next stitch on left needle.
  With right needle, knit into the front of this loop.
  To make this increase on the purl side, insert left needle in same manner and purl into the front of the loop.

Make 1 with Backward Loop over the right needle
With your thumb, make a loop over the right needle.
Slip the loop from your thumb onto the needle and pull to tighten.

Make 1 in top of stitch below
Insert tip of right needle into the stitch on left needle one row below.
  Knit this stitch, then knit the stitch on the left needle.

Decrease (dec)

Knit 2 together (k2tog)
Put tip of right needle through next two stitches on left needle as to knit. Knit these two stitches as one.

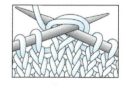

Purl 2 together (p2tog)
Put tip of right needle through next two stitches on left needle as to purl. Purl these two stitches as one.

Slip, Slip, Knit (ssk)
Slip next two stitches, one at a time, as to knit from left needle to right needle.
  Insert left needle in front of both stitches and work off needle together.

Slip, Slip, Purl (ssp)
Slip next two stitches, one at a time, as to knit from left needle to right needle. Slip these stitches back onto left needle keeping them twisted. Purl these two stitches together through back loops.

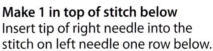

Crochet Basics

Some knit items are finished with a crochet trim or edging. Below are some abbreviations used in crochet and a review of some basic crochet stitches.

Chain Stitch (ch)
Begin by making a slip knot on the hook. Bring the yarn over the hook from back to front and draw through the loop on the hook.

For each additional chain stitch, bring the yarn over the hook from back to front and draw through the loop on the hook.

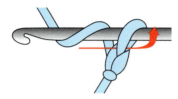

Slip Stitch (sl st)
Insert hook under both loops of the stitch, bring yarn over the hook from back to front and draw it through the stitch and the loop on the hook.

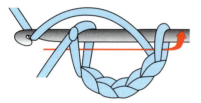

Half Double Crochet (hdc)
Yo, insert hook in st, yo, pull through st, yo, pull through all 3 lps on hook.

Single Crochet (sc)
Insert the hook in the second chain through the center of the V. Bring the yarn over the hook from back to front.

Draw the yarn through the chain stitch and onto the hook.

Again bring yarn over the hook from back to front and draw it through both loops on hook.

For additional rows of single crochet, insert the hook under both loops of the previous stitch instead of through the center of the V as when working into the chain stitch.

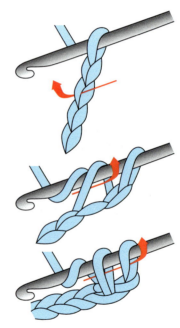

Knitting Techniques

Knitted Cast-On

This is an easy beginning, worked with two needles and one strand of yarn. Knit Tip: If you have trouble with a too-tight edge, try using a slightly larger needle to cast on, then change to the size you need to obtain the gauge.

1. Make a slip knot on left needle. Insert tip of right needle into slip knot (loop).

2. Knit 1 in loop.

3. Without sliding previous loop off, place new stitch on left needle.

4. Repeat steps 2 and 3 until desired number of stitches is cast on.

Kitchener Stitch

This method of weaving with two needles is used for the toes of socks and flat seams. To weave the edges together and form an unbroken line of stockinette stitch, divide all stitches evenly onto two knitting needles—one behind the other. Thread yarn into tapestry needle. Hold needles with wrong sides together and work from right to left as follows:

Step 1: Insert tapestry needle into first stitch on front needle as to purl. Draw yarn through stitch, leaving stitch on knitting needle.

Step 2: Insert tapestry needle into the first stitch on the back needle as to purl. Draw yarn through stitch and slip stitch off knitting needle.

Step 3: Insert tapestry needle into the next stitch on same (back) needle as to knit, leaving stitch on knitting needle.

Step 4: Insert tapestry needle into the first stitch on the front needle as to knit. Draw yarn through stitch and slip stitch off knitting needle.

Step 5: Insert tapestry needle into the next stitch on same (front) needle as to purl. Draw yarn through stitch, leaving stitch on knitting needle.

Repeat Steps 2–5 until 1 stitch is left on each needle. Then repeat Steps 2 and 4. Fasten off. Woven stitches should be the same size as adjacent knitted stitches.

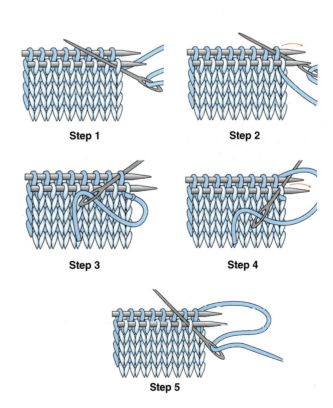

Felting & Embroidery

The Felt Formula
Felting is not a precise science. Wool felts when exposed to water, heat and agitation, but each element is hard to control precisely. As a result, each individual project may vary in the way it felts.

Felting can be done in the sink, but washing machines get the job done more quickly. Each washing machine is different, and the rate at which specific machines felt a piece will vary. So, be sure to follow the specific felting instructions of the piece you are making, and check your piece several times during the felting process to make sure you are getting the desired results.

The felting process releases fibers which can clog your washing machine. Therefore, you may want to place items in a zippered pillowcase before putting them in the washing machine. Also, adding other laundry, such as jeans, when felting will increase the amount of agitation and speed up the process. Be careful not to use items that shed fibers of their own, such as towels.

Felting Facts
Felting a knit or crochet piece makes it shrink. Therefore, the piece you knit must start out much larger than the finished felted size will be. Shrinkage varies because there are so many factors that affect it. These variables include water temperature, the hardness of the water, how much (and how long) the piece is agitated, the amount and type of soap used, yarn brand, fiber content and color.

You can control how much your piece felts by watching it closely. Check your piece after about 10 minutes to see how quickly it is felting. Look at the stitch definition and size to determine if the piece has been felted enough.

How to Felt
Place items to be felted in the washing machine along with one tablespoon of dish detergent and a pair of jeans or other laundry. (Remember, do not felt projects with other clothing that release their own fibers.) Set washing machine on smallest load and use hot water. Start machine and check progress after ten minutes. Check progress more frequently after piece starts to felt. Reset the machine if needed to continue the agitation cycle. Do not allow machine to go to spin cycle; rapid spinning can cause creases in the felted fabric that may be very difficult to get out later. As the piece becomes more felted, you may need to pull it into shape.

When the piece has felted to the desired size, rinse it by hand in warm water. Remove the excess water by rolling in a towel and squeezing.

Block the piece into shape, and let air dry. Do not dry in clothes dryer. For pieces that need to conform to a particular shape (such as a hat or purse), stuff the piece with a towel to help it hold its shape while drying. Felted items are very strong, so don't be afraid to push and pull them into the desired shapes. It may take several hours or several days for the pieces to dry completely.

After the piece is completely dry, excess fuzziness can be trimmed with scissors if a smoother surface is desired, or the piece can be brushed for a fuzzier appearance.

Embroidery Stitches

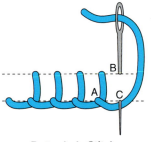

Buttonhole Stitch

Chain Stitch

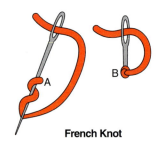

French Knot

Special Techniques

Working in the Round

Working With Double-Point Needles

Helpful Tips:
Make sure that the cast on edge remains along the inside of the circle on each needle. This will help prevent the stitches from twisting around the needles.

Slip the first cast-on stitch from the left-hand needle tip to the right-hand needle tip. Slip the last cast-on stitch from the right-hand needle tip up and over the stitch just transferred and onto the left-hand needle tip to "join" into a ring.

4 Double-Point Needles

Cast on the number of stitches required. Distribute the stitches as instructed in the pattern on 3 double-point needles. Position the needles so that needle 1 is on the left and needle 3 is on the right. The yarn you're about to work with should be attached to the last stitch on needle 3.

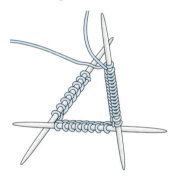
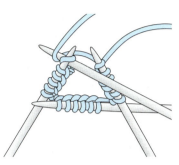

5 Double-Point Needles

Cast on the number of stitches required. Distribute stitches evenly on 4 double-point needles. Position the needles so that needle 1 is on the left and needle 4 is on the right. The yarn you're about to work with should be attached to the last stitch on needle 4.

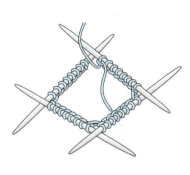

Intarsia

In certain patterns there are larger areas of color within the piece. Since this type of pattern requires a new color only for that section, it is not necessary to carry the yarn back and forth across the back. For this type of color change, a separate ball of yarn or bobbin is used for each color, making the yarn available only where needed. Bring the new yarn being used up-and-around the yarn just worked; this will "lock" the colors and prevent holes from occurring at the join.

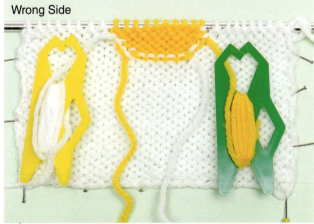

Seam Finishes

Mattress Seam

This type of seam can be used for vertical seams (like side seams). It is worked with the right sides of the pieces facing you, making it easier to match stitches for stripe patterns. It is worked between the first and second stitch at the edge of the piece and works best when the first stitch is a selvage stitch.

To work this seam, thread a tapestry needle with matching yarn. Insert the needle into one corner of work from back to front, just above the cast on stitch, leaving a 3-inch tail. Take needle to edge of other piece and bring it from back to front at the corner of this piece.

Return to the first piece and insert the needle from the right to wrong side where the thread comes out of the piece. Slip the needle upward under one horizontal thread and bring the needle through to the right side.

Cross to the other side and repeat the same process "down where you came out, under one thread and up."

Continue working back and forth on the two pieces in the same manner for about an inch, then gently pull on the thread pulling the two pieces together. (Photo A)

Complete the seam and fasten off. Use the beginning tail to even-up the lower edge by working a figure 8 between the cast-on stitches at the corners. Insert the threaded needle from front to back under both threads of the corner cast-on stitch on the edge opposite the tail, then into the same stitch on the

Photo A

Photo B

first edge. Pull gently until the figure 8 fills the gap. (Photo B)

When a project is made with a textured yarn that will not pull easily through the pieces, it is recommended that a smooth yarn of the same color be used to work the seam.

Garter Stitch Seams

The "bumps" of the garter stitch selvage nestle between each other in a garter stitch seam, often producing a nearly reversible seam. This is a good seam for afghan strips and blocks of the same color. Starting as for the mattress seam, work from bump to bump, alternating sides. In this case you enter each stitch only once.

3-Needle Bind-Off

Use this technique for seaming two edges together, such as when joining a seam. Hold the live edge stitches on two separate needles with right sides of the fabric together.

With a third needle, knit together a stitch from the front needle with one from the back.

Repeat, knitting a stitch from the front needle with one from the back needle once more.

Slip the first stitch over the second.

Repeat knitting, a front and back pair of stitches together, then bind one pair off.

Matching Patterns

When it comes to matching stripes and other elements in a design, a simple formula makes things line up perfectly:

Begin the seam in the usual way.

Enter the first stitch of each new color stripe (or pattern detail) on the same side as you began the seam; i.e. the same side as your tail.

Knitting With Beads

Threading beads onto yarn is the most common way to knit with beads.

Step 1: Before beginning to knit, thread the beads onto your skein of yarn using a bead threader. As you work, unwind a small quantity of yarn, each time sliding the beads towards the ball until needed. Pass the yarn through the loop of the threader and pick up beads with the working end of the needle.

Step 2: Slide the beads over the loop and onto the yarn.

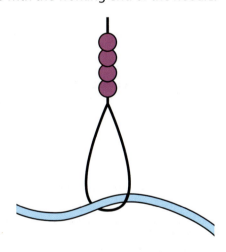

Knitting Needle Conversion Chart

U.S.	1	2	3	4	5	6	7	8	9	10	10½	11	13	15	17	19	35	50
Continental-mm	2.25	2.75	3.25	3.5	3.75	4	4.5	5	5.5	6	6.5	8	9	10	12	15	19	25

Inches into Millimetres & Centimetres

All measurements are rounded off slightly.

inches	mm	cm	inches	cm	inches	cm	inches	cm	inches	cm
⅛	3	0.3	3	7.5	13	33.0	26	66.0	39	99.0
¼	6	0.6	3½	9.0	14	35.5	27	68.5	40	101.5
⅜	10	1.0	4	10.0	15	38.0	28	71.0	41	104.0
½	13	1.3	4½	11.5	16	40.5	29	73.5	42	106.5
⅝	15	1.5	5	12.5	17	43.0	30	76.0	43	109.0
¾	20	2.0	5½	14	18	46.0	31	79.0	44	112.0
⅞	22	2.2	6	15.0	19	48.5	32	81.5	45	114.5
1	25	2.5	7	18.0	20	51.0	33	84.0	46	117.0
1¼	32	3.8	8	20.5	21	53.5	34	86.5	47	119.5
1½	38	3.8	9	23.0	22	56.0	35	89.0	48	122.0
1¾	45	4.5	10	25.5	23	58.5	36	91.5	49	124.5
2	50	5.0	11	28.0	24	61.0	37	94.0	50	127.0
2½	65	6.5	12	30.5	25	63.5	38	96.5		

Standard Yarn Weight System

Categories of yarn, gauge ranges and recommended needle sizes

Yarn Weight Symbol & Category Names	1 SUPER FINE	2 FINE	3 LIGHT	4 MEDIUM	5 BULKY	6 SUPER BULKY
Type of Yarns in Category	Sock, Fingering, Baby	Sport, Baby	DK, Light Worsted	Worsted, Afghan, Aran	Chunky, Craft, Rug	Super Chunky, Roving
Knit Gauge Range* in Stockinette Stitch to 4 inches	27–32 sts	23–26 sts	21–24 sts	16–20 sts	12–15 sts	6–11 sts
Recommended Needle in Metric Size Range	2.25–3.25mm	3.25–3.75mm	3.75–4.5mm	4.5–5.5mm	5.5–8mm	8mm and larger
Recommended Needle U.S. Size Range	1 to 3	3 to 5	5 to 7	7 to 9	9 to 11	11 and larger

* **GUIDELINES ONLY:** The above reflect the most commonly used gauges and needle sizes for specific yarn categories.

Skill Levels

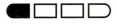
BEGINNER

Beginner projects for first-time knitters using basic stitches. Minimal shaping.

EASY

Easy projects using basic stitches, repetitive stitch patterns, simple color changes, and simple shaping and finishing.

INTERMEDIATE

Intermediate projects with a variety of stitches, mid-level shaping and finishing.

EXPERIENCED

Experienced projects using advanced techniques and stitches, detailed shaping and refined finishing.

In the Nick of Time is published by DRG, 306 East Parr Road, Berne, IN 46711. Printed in USA. Copyright © 2010 DRG. All rights reserved. This publication may not be reproduced in part or in whole without written permission from the publisher.

RETAIL STORES: If you would like to carry this pattern book or any other DRG publications, visit DRGwholesale.com

Every effort has been made to ensure that the instructions in this pattern book are complete and accurate. We cannot, however, take responsibility for human error, typographical mistakes or variations in individual work. Please visit AnniesCustomerCare.com to check for pattern updates.

ISBN: 978-1-59217-303-7

2 3 4 5 6 7 8

House of White Birches, Berne, Indiana 46711   AnniesAttic.com

Photo Index

47

17

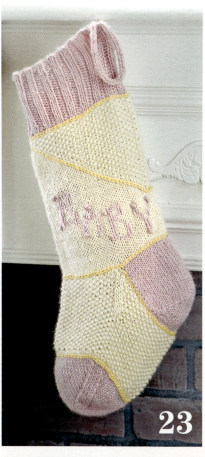

23

31

27

House of White Birches, Berne, Indiana 46711   AnniesAttic.com